D1577985

CUBA

BY
EDDY KOHLI

a voyage in images

He felt tired; he had run out of ideas. And he was waiting for a phone call that never seemed to arrive. Maybe it was because of that endless delay: an unhappiness as light as silk filtered into his soul. He got up from the desk where he had been trying to complete an article that seemed to resist all efforts to pin it down, to find a good ending, and he walked over to the window. The window: a harmonious midway point between the indoors and the outdoors, between the self and the city, the confusion, the welter of sounds that was impossible to decipher.

The silhouettes of the buildings were growing gray. The day was verging on sunset, slowly. Slowly: the exponential speed of his life, dominated by an ironbound grid of dates and deadlines, had always kept him from stopping, from having time to think calmly. In this he was no different from everyone else, perhaps. And now, suddenly, in that minuscule moment, hidden in the drab gray of the evening, he was aware of something new. Without his notice, time had accumulated on things like a transparent film. What he was feeling was, perhaps, something more than just exhaustion. He was growing old. It was as if the vital energy of youth was slowly trickling away.

The slow inching of the shadows, extending imperceptibly, was actually marking his own private sunset. It seemed to him that the wave of darkness that was filling the streets was pushing him willy-nilly toward the final, closing chapter of life. He had been kidding himself. He had believed that he was moving in an absolute continuum, free of all the chains of time—but that had collapsed now. And in this, too, perhaps, he was no different from everyone else. He was unable to capture the essence of time, and he was drifting helplessly toward distant lands—as if the wind had suddenly dropped, leaving him in the doldrums, in unknown waters.

The phone rang just as he was floating in this melancholy limbo. It was his editor at the newspaper: "Are you interested in taking a holiday in the tropics? In just a couple of days, you are leaving for Cuba. Destination: la Isla de la Juventud, the Island of Youth. I am not sure where it is—check the atlas. There is a young Cuban woman named Deborah something-or-other who is about to break some world record for breath-held diving. In the photographs, this woman looks to be a genuine, blonde mermaid. I am absolutely indifferent to her athletic records—tell me about this person. Why the silence? Why don't you answer me?"

"Got it," he answered. "Okay." He had never been to Cuba and he had never heard of the Island of Youth. But the word youth made an impression on him. Precisely when, tangled in the usual existential toils, he had glimpsed the furthest point of the horizon and sensed the frequency of the shadows, destiny was propelling him elsewhere, into a sudden burst of light. The gravitational forces of being: absurd and perfectly logical. But why the Island of Youth?

Seventy-two hours later, he found himself at the antipodes of his world. Framed in the window, the landscape had changed completely. The brilliant, hot sunlight had burnt away the shadows of sunset. In the dazzling light of the Caribbean, every last fragment of nature stood out sharply and clearly. The evanescent shapes of sunset in the city were taking new form in the virgin splendor of an exotic dawn. Even the white shapes of the Hotel Colony, the only tourist accommodations in the luxuriant wilderness of the little Isla de la Juventud, seemed to be made of solidified light. And he had a feeling that the light was surging into the labyrinth of his mind, restoring it, rejuvenating it.

Early the next morning, he was climbing on board the boat of the champion diver—"the queen of the depths," as she had been dubbed by *Granma*, the newspaper of the Cuban Communist Party—and while she was paddling off with her escort of scuba divers, he enjoyed the view of the still, blue waters of the Caribbean. Every time the motorboat moved, he had the distinct impression that he was further shattering the few bonds that remained with the land and with his own past. The fabulous expanse of the sea (the same "ever-changing topaz sea" that he had learned to love through the writing of Gabriel García Márquez) was triggering a vast array of interior echoes. It was as if, at this latitude, the spiral of time was unfolding with a strange kind of slowness.

One morning, he even experienced the thrill of danger. He dove with the scuba team to watch Deborah in action. The water was transparent, a sort of cobalt blue. Through his diving mask he could just see the beginning of the abyss.

Then, suddenly, something happened. A long silhouette, the color of steel, appeared in the crystalline water. One hardly needed to be an experienced diver to guess this new threat: it was a shark. It glided past him at a distance of only a few yards. It must have been ten feet long. And yet he was not afraid. At that moment, he felt nothing but curiosity. The shark drew close to the scuba diver who was monitoring Deborah at the bottom of her dive, and then suddenly disappeared into the blue, like a phantom. "Too bad," he thought. A few minutes later, the phantom reappeared below him. Slowly, it was climbing toward the surface, tracing concentric circles around the cable that anchored the boat to the sea bottom. Deborah's trainer, who was floating at a depth of fifteen or twenty yards, made a clearly understandable sign with his hands: the shark is hungry, everyone out of the water. With the others, he rose, almost reluctantly. On the surface, the sea was a mosaic of colored tiles.

During that first trip he barely got a glimpse of Havana. And yet, even though he stayed far from the capital of "Socialismo o Muerte," and was confined to a Garden of Earthly Delights, he had opportunities to plumb the complexity of the mysteries of Cuba. It was Deborah who, unintentionally, gave him the access key. One evening, as they were having a drink together on the beach of the Hotel Colony, comfortably seated in the shadows of the palm trees, as the sinking sun spread out into a patch of fire-red light, she told him about the major chapters of her life.

She was twenty-eight years old; her family was of Spanish origin. Her father had been a general, "a classic revolucionario," a member of the Central Committee, and the right-hand man of Fidel Castro's brother Raul. Her mother, Cuqui, was quite religious. She had been a member of the Catholic church prior to the Revolution; then she had to reject her religion because it was forbidden; and then, after she separated from her husband, she began to practice it once again. Deborah told him nothing of her brother, but someone else filled him in on the secret: at the age of nineteen he had fled to Florida with the first waves of *balseros*, or Cuban boat people. It had been a terrible blow for the entire family. She told him only, "I am never tempted to abandon this island. Whenever I am away even for a short time, I get terribly homesick. Cuba is more than just the place where I was born, it is my home. I could never give up its nature and its beauty. The people of Cuba are great creators of confusion, but even confusion has its positive aspects."

When, after one week, it was time for him to leave, he felt a surge of sadness. During those seven endless days, he had felt his obsession with speed slip away. Now, as his plane was soaring back over the Atlantic Ocean, he once again had a sense of being extraneous, of not belonging. It seemed to him that he was heading for an uncertain destination—the same old feeling. What was more, he felt as if he had broken off a conversation in the middle. He had only begun to delve into the mysteries of Cuba, and here he was heading home again.

The image that he had formed of the island was a concentrate of stereotypes: Hemingway and the Gulf Stream, salsa and daiquiris, white beaches and lush palms, "Our Man in Havana," *santeria*, the *barbudos* of the Sierra Maestra, and the austere icon of Che Guevara with a cigar dangling from his lip. He knew perfectly well that it was a false image, something from a postcard, and that Cuba was not what it seemed—a Happy Isle; all the same, he continued to think back on it, and often.

In the evenings, as he looked out his window, stopping to observe the frenetic passage of life in the city, unsure as always about how to end his articles, and uncertain about the meaning of his own existential sunset, his mind would return to that vision of a blessed isle, bathed in the purest sunlight, where time had somehow been tamed and people were in love with slowness.

Over time, Cuba (along with the little Isla de la Juventud) crystallized in an apparently unattainable distance in space and time. And then one day, as he was chewing over one of his countless unsolvable knots, in the crepuscular light he once again glimpsed the shape of his mysterious island.

The editor spoke firmly over the phone: "This time, I want real reporting. I want to know what is really happening on that island. Is it true that the American embargo is starving Cuba, or it that just a fable of propaganda? Why do some tourists come back thrilled, wearing Che Guevara t-shirts, and others tell of a land haunted by poverty and prostitution? In other words, why has Communism collapsed everywhere else, but it holds out in Cuba?"

"Okay," he answered, taciturn as ever. And so, Cuba appeared on his horizon, just as it had the first time. The phone rang, and a few hours later he was flying over the ocean into a beautiful and ever-changing world, described by journalists as being "in transition," although none of them could ever describe the direction of that transition—any more than he could give an answer to that last question. He was fully aware of that: what right did he have to attempt to reveal an answer that had remained a mystery for forty years, ever since the guerrillas of the Sierra Maestra entered the city of Havana in triumph in January 1959? But he chose to continue the effort.

As he rode in the taxi from the airport to the hotel in the center of Havana, he remembered something Deborah had said: "I feel as if the sea belongs to a superior being that is capable of protecting or destroying. And so, every time I am about to dive, I say silently: 'Forgive me, I ask permission to enter your kingdom.' Then I take seven small coins, seven *centavos*, and I toss them into the water."

It had just stopped raining—a tropical downpour. The trees were wreathed in a pearly steam. He put his hand in his pocket and dug out seven *centavos*. He grasped them in his hand, and at the first stop light, tossed them out the window of the taxi into a puddle.

A few minutes later, the taxi drove into a chaotic and rundown city: Havana. The sun had come out again, a garish sun, and smiling people were streaming toward the Malecón, the long beach that lies at the heart of the dreams of every Cuban. The water glittered like a great sheet of satin. Time seemed to pass in slow motion.

When he walked out of the hotel in the evening, a tall old man approached him. The man had a knife-sharp face, with a serene, remote expression. He introduced himself: "My name is Antonio. I am retired, though I have no pension. I live alone not far from here, in Habana Vieja, and I would like to talk with a foreigner. Do you have some time to spare?"

They sat on a bench. Antonio said he was a writer, and added that he was "finishing a book of profound ideas," entitled *Dialogos Oniricos*. They talked for a long time. Before taking his leave, the old man asked if he had a piece of paper. He wanted to write down a thought he had been mulling over for a long time. He handed the old man his notebook. Antonio wrote, in a fine hand: 'Every man is a prisoner of two infinite prisons, time and space. So why hurry? It makes no sense to hurry unless it is absolutely necessary.'

Massimo Dini

Stretched out
in the boat
bringing him
to Havana,
Santiago—
the fisherman
of *The Old Man
and the Sea*—
strains
to see
the glowing
halo
of the
city lights.
"They were only
perceptible
at first
as the light is
in the sky
before
the moon
rises."
Images of a
city
that seems
at the point
of vanishing,
a will-o'-the-
wisp hovering
in the air.
In Havana
begins
this
photographic
itinerary that
traces the
length of the
island,
being neither
a traveler's
journal
nor (abominable
idea!)
a guide to be
followed.
It is
the portrait of
a place,
composed of
the innumerable
portaits
of the
people the
photographer
has met—
the portrait
of a love.
Mea Cuba.

A joke is making the rounds these days in Cuba. A man asks a boy, "What would you like to be when you grow up?" The boy answers, "A tourist."

"Lorca sees what he calls 'the most beautiful women in the world' in Havana/ and then the celebration demands explanation: 'This island is a paradise. If you lose me, look for me in Cuba.'"

Guillermo Cabrera Infante

My hands
are empty/
They always
give when
there's
nothing to
give/
Oh, but
what's to
be done/
They're the
only hands
I've got."
These
verses of
the
songwriter
Juan
Formell
portray the
generosity
that is
typical of
Cubans,
among whom
'miser'
is the
worst
possible
insult.

Black beans, white rice: nicknamed *moros y christianos*, this staple accompanies any dish in the simple cooking of the *campo*, the Cuban countryside.

Locals can even fish on El Malecón, the main street of Havana: its five kilometers follow the shoreline as far as El Vedado.

Voodoo has its origins with the Yoruba of Africa. It learned to dissimulate its gods (*orishas*) as Christian saints to avoid accusations of heresy.

CRISTAL

PARTICULAR
HM·68060
CUBA

A dancer with a spectacularly illuminated headdress at the Tropicana. Founded in 1931 and kept open even during the harshest years of the revolution, Havana's most famous nightclub is open to the air, ringed by a thick stand of tropical trees with neon flickering among the foliage. The Tropicana always shines, even when a blackout sinks the rest of the city into darkness.

The ground floors of old colonial houses often contain small shops, amid remains of past splendor.

"The pilasters...of what had once been the aristocratic quarter were eroded like coral.... to the west rose the steel skyscrapers of the new city."

Graham Greene

The youngest wing of the Communist Party. Every schoolchild between the age of 5 and 15 is part of the party.

The effect of the revolution on marriage has been to increase the rate of divorce. In 1953, 1 out of 19 marriages ended in divorce. In 1990 the figure increased to 2 out of 3.

Starting in 1961, the year of the embargo by the United States, no new parts arrived. Only the meticulous care of the mechanics prevented these authentic models from going to pieces.

They are called "the figs of Adam," the small green bananas, plantains, that in the years of the food ration card helped replace pork and other meat. Talent taught how to satisfy one's whims in their preparation; the plantian can be fried in strips when unripe, and it can be cooked whole when ripe. It is also possible to boil large pieces, crushing them with a fork and adding pieces of fried pork and oil for an African flavor. A type of culinary obsession pervades everything, from language to music. Today one sings a song about an incautious goat who, after going to a party, finds himself as stewed meat, but in the forties Benny Moreno dedicated a passage directly to a little pig.

Cuba is a thread of smoke, strong, mellow, dense. Cuba is its cigars and its tobacco. The first, central leaf (*tripa*) gives shape to the cigar; the second holds it together (*hoja de fortalezza*); the third, called *de combustion*, guarantees that the cigar will light. And the last, *la colpa*, envelops the whole, secured with a light glue of rice. Every two minutes an expert worker rolls a cigar. And during the day a 'reader', from his post in the main hall, reads the newspapers in the morning and a story in the afternoon. This tradition arose in the 19th century, and contributed in its way to the war of independence, as condemnations of Spanish power became favorite readings in the factories. José Martí, the hero of the war against the colonizers, used this method to keep even cigar workers in Florida informed of the national uprising. It was a short step from awareness to solidarity, and ten percent of each worker's salary began to flow regularly into the coffers of the movement.

The finest tobacco leaves are collected to the west of Havana, in the district of Vuelta Abajo.

To encourage his countrymen to mind their health, Fidel Castro has become the first and perhaps the only Cuban to give up cigars.

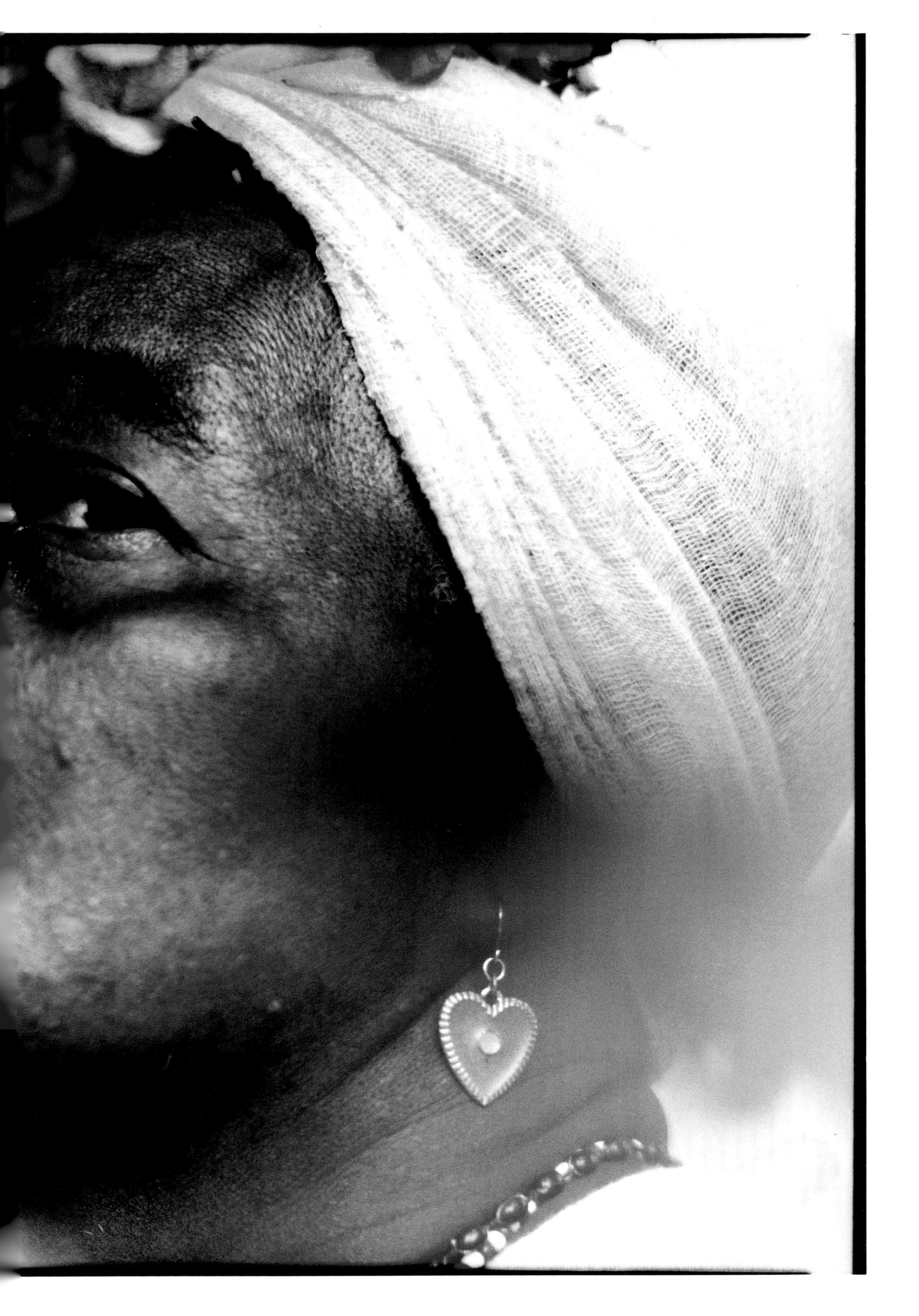

"I went to Santiago...Caiman.... Tobacco flower

I HAVE ALWAYS SAID THAT I WENT TO SANTIAGO IN A CARRIAGE OF BLACK WATER." GARCIA LORCA

Drilling Plants.
The collapse of the USSR in 1991 had devastating effects, abolishing economic aid and reducing commercial relationships. One of the gravest consequences was the scarcity of oil.

"The heads of the palms sing...O rhythm of dry branches...Harp of living trunks"
Federico García Lorca

"Beautiful faces looked out of the dark caverns, Spanish and smooth-skinned black."

Graham Greene

In 1959,
the year of
the triumph of
the revolution,
1.5% of Cuban
landowners
held nearly
half of all
cultivated
fields, and
two-thirds
of all
agricultural
workers
were landless
day laborers.
"We have today
decided
to come
to the
plantation
and destroy
it....
The Rebel Army
is ready
to carry
agrarian
reform to its
ultimate
conclusion.
But the land
that the
people have
seized will not
see a single
commander of
our forces;
not a single
soldier of
this army
will raise arms
against the
peasants,
our friends
forever."

Ignacio Paco Taibo II,
quoting Che Guevara

ULTIMATE
XR
ULTIMATE
XR

"Living in Havana was like living in a factory that produced human beauty on an assembly line."

Graham Greene

Resolver: to get out of it, to make do. Every Cuban, with 15 liters of gas to use each month

(WHEN THERE IS GAS AT ALL), IS WILLING TO BOARD ANYTHING WITH WHEELS IN ORDER TO GET AROUND.

Fighting cocks are raised with all possible care. They train, (wearing muzzles, to avoid hurting

THEMSELVES) EVERY MORNING, STARTING AT DAWN.

Children, the pride of Cuba: its infant mortality rate is among the world's twenty lowest.

"There are certain cities, strange at first sight, which are closer to the heart than the family hearth... Drawing near Havana in the early morning... looking at the green-silver color of the island rising from the sea, I had the premonition that what I was about to see would hold singular importance for me.... It was as if a fascinating dream had become solid.... I heard then the voice of Havana, a staccato voice notable because, as I was to learn, it never lapses into calm."

Joseph Hergesheimer

Beer and rum are the national drinks of Cuba. Lager beer, cold beer, pure and transparent for the Free Cuba (with Coca-Cola), for the Saoco (with cold milk), for the Daiquiri, which Ernest Hemingway used to drink in Florida, where today, on his favorite chair, there is a bust in his likeness. The writer was loved by the Cubans for his literary talent and for his talent in choice of cocktail.

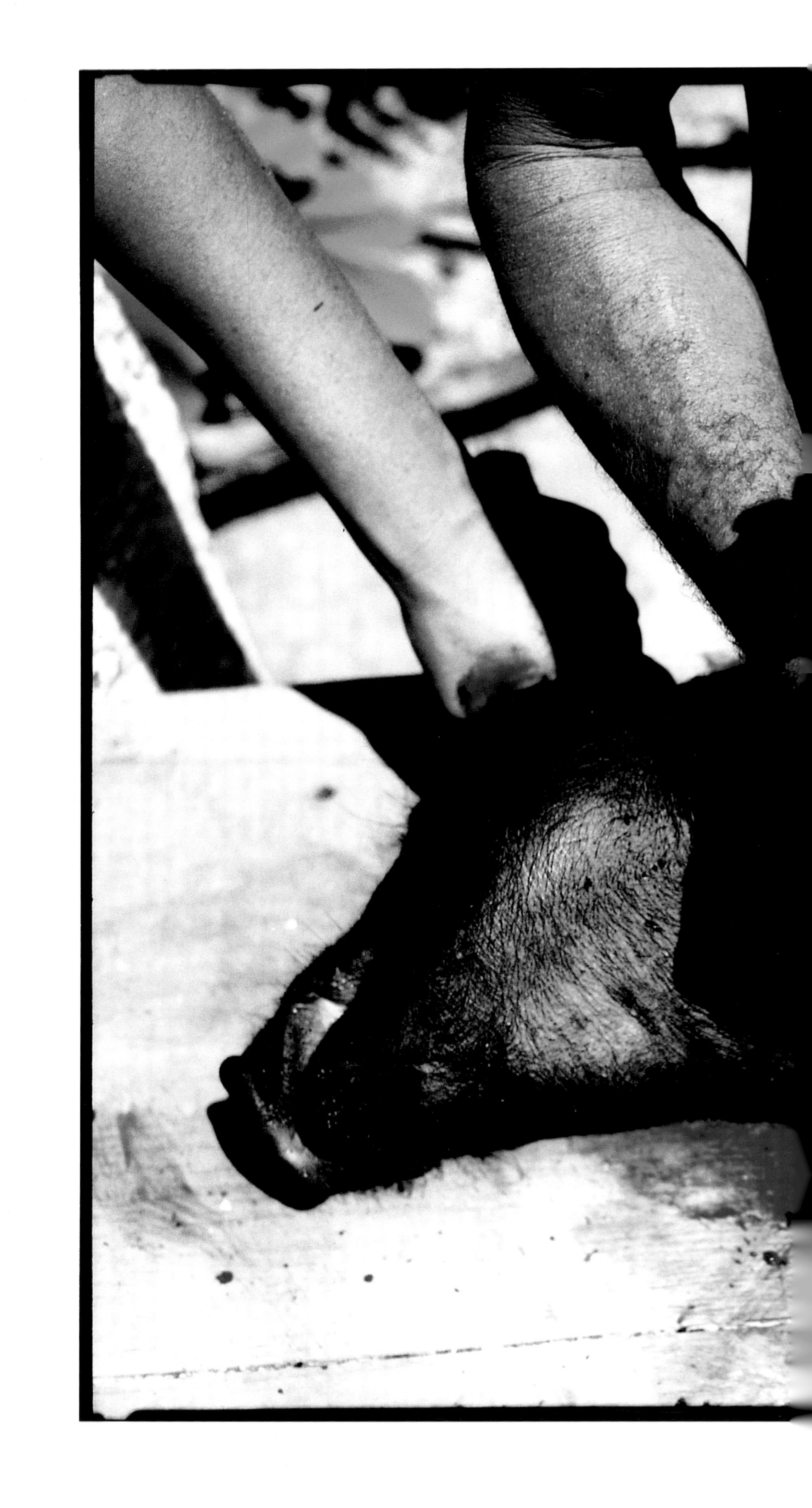

Pork is the foundation of Cuban cuisine. Without pork, the classic *criollo* plate is reduced to a motley vegetarian dish of rice and beans, yucca, and fried banana slices. Pork gives perfume, body, and cheer: it is the dish of *noche buona*, Christmas Eve. Beef has become extremely scarce, and is not bought more than two or three times a year—but always on May Day and on the 26th of July, the anniversary of Castro's attack on the Moncada barracks.

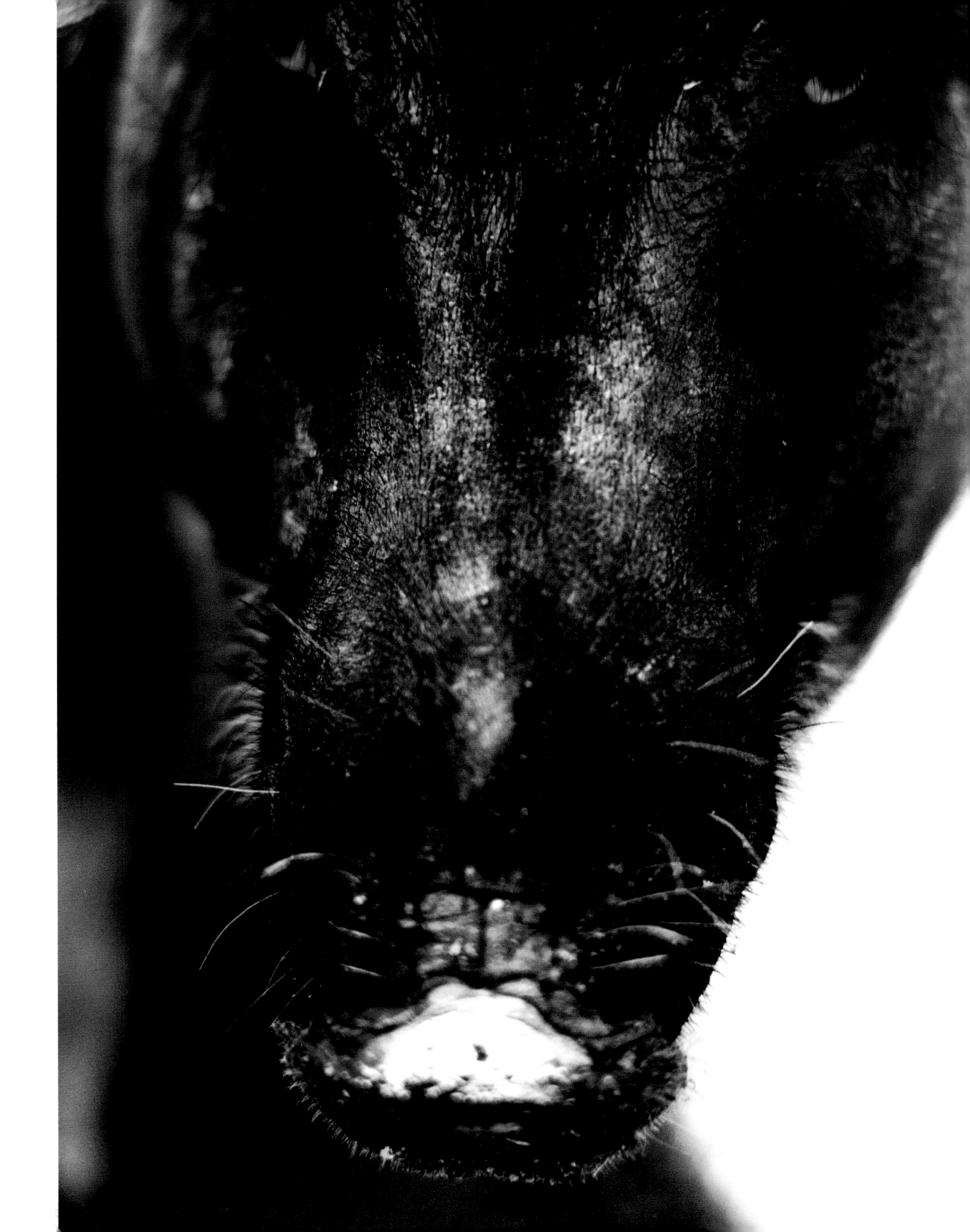

Green Cuba: a thousand species of insects (here, a centipede), 185 species of butterfly, 350 species of birds, among which the tocororo (*Priotelus temnurus*) is considered the national symbol, 38 species of mammals, and 6000 of plants.

"But there was a serenity, a quiet that I have found nowhere else. In this state of fullness, one of the most ineffable, intense moments was the lifting of the fog."

Reinaldo Arenas

Monteros (cowboys) are the men for whom the immense territory of Cuba holds no secrets.

At right: A lake in the forest of Pinar del Rio province.

An always-changing landscape opens before your eyes as you ascend the Curanagaia waterfall.

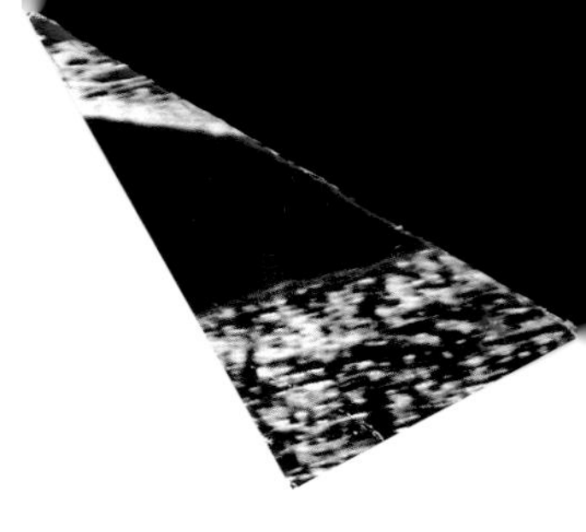

THE *GUAJIROS*, SMALL FARMERS, ARE DESCENDED FROM THE COLONISTS WHO, IN THE BEGINNING OF THE 18TH CENTURY, REBELLED AGAINST THE SPANISH MONOPOLY. THE CELEBRATED BALLAD "GUATANAMERA" IS DEDICATED TO THESE EARLY HEROES.

Sugar, the white gold, has always been the motor of the Cuban economy; *La Zafra*, the harvest, is today conducted by hand for want of tractor fuel.

Old American cars are cherished treasures. In Havana there is even a museum dedicated to the relics of mid-century, among which shines Che Guevara's Chevy.

"At the Tropicana ...Dancers three meters high perform between the large palms."
Graham Greene

The *roqeros* (from the English 'rocker') are a thorn in the side of the government, which accuses them of being antisocial, and of the police, who persecute them with raids and arrests.

Cuba consists of 10 million inhabitants, the largest percentage of whom are mestizo, followed by a mixture of ethnicities: African, European, native, and Chinese.

"OUR GOAL WAS ALWAYS THE SEA, FOREVER AND HOWEVER. THE SEA, A FESTIVAL WHICH OBLIGED US

Cuba consists of 10 million inhabitants, the largest percentage of whom are mestizo, followed by a mixture of ethnicities: African, European, Native, and Chinese.

Underwood

In Santiago, the "heroic city" where Castro accepted the surrender of Battista's army in 1959, an old typewriter has the eloquence of involuntary symbolism. Described, recounted, imagined, transfigured, remembered by the exiles with the nostalgia of desperation, cursed, dreamed, Cuba became a pure place for literature. From the time Hemingway lit his Corona and began *To Have and Have Not*: Do you know how the morning is in Havana, with the vagabonds still sleeping along the walls, before the ice vans begin their trips to the bars?

"Our goal was always the sea, forever and however. The sea, a festival which obliged us

TO BE JOYFUL EVEN WHEN WE DIDN'T WANT TO." Reinaldo Arenas

LUCA SIGNORELLI

PRODUCER
FABIO FASOLINI

EXECUTIVE PRODUCERS
CRISTINA MANTOVANI
NAIMA ZEGHLOUL

RESEARCH, COORDINATION, AND ORGANIZATION IN CUBA
ROMAN FERNANDEZ

PRODUCTION COORDINATION IN CUBA
SATO DI BENEDETTO
CORRADO POZZOLI

GRAPHIC DESIGN
PIERPAOLO PITACCO

PROJECT DEVELOPMENT
BRUNA ROSSI

EDITORIAL CONSULTATION
LUIGI GIANNUZZI

TEXT EDITOR
GIUSI FERRE

WITH THANKS TO

FILM
KODAK FILM

ORIGINAL DEVELOPING AND PRINTING
IMAGE - SIPANE LAB - PARIGI
TRAVEL ARRANGEMENTS
VIAGGI CORTESIA SRL - MILANO

MINISTRY OF TOURISM OF CUBA
MINISTRY OF CULTURE OF CUBA
MINISTRY OF ART AND ENTERTAINMENT OF CUBA

Sources:

Ernest Hemingway
To Have and Have Not

Ernest Hemingway
The Old Man and the Sea

Graham Greene
Our Man in Havana

Paco Ignacio Taibo
Without Losing Tenderness

Reinaldo Arenas
Before Night Falls

Guanda Guillermo Cabrera Infante
My Cuba

Norberto Fuentes
Hemingway in Cuba

Joseph Hergesheimer
San Cristobal de la Habana

Federico García Lorca
Poems

First published in the United States of America in 1997 by
RIZZOLI INTERNATIONAL PUBLICATIONS, INC.
300 Park Avenue South, New York, NY 10010

Cuba was prepared and produced by
STUDIO F.P. Srl
Via Revere 7
20123 Milan

ISBN 0-8478-2065-3
LC 97-66476

Introduction translated by Tony Shugaar

Printed in Italy by Grafiche Milani